THE WALK SHE TAKES

THE
WALK
SHE
TAKES

Neile Graham

MoonPath Press

Poetry
ISBN 978-1-936657-47-6

Cover photo of Ring of Brodgar by Neile Graham

Author photo by Leslie Howle

Book design by Tonya Namura using Adobe Jenson Pro

MoonPath Press is dedicated to publishing the finest poets
living in the U.S. Pacific Northwest.

MoonPath Press
PO Box 445
Tillamook, OR 97141

MoonPathPress@gmail.com

http://MoonPathPress.com

For my father, John Barclay Graham, 1926–2015
and every word for Jim

Table of Contents

THE
WALK
SHE
TAKES

Border Country

3 St Ronan's Drive

in another life I still own my third of this house
my own piece of Scotland
I've bought out my sister and the Swansea cousin
reversed the tide of immigration
New World to Old
voyaged east, backwards
to undo my grandparents' journey
—I too on that boat meet my future all unknowing—

instead when the house was so briefly so partially
mine I'd already entered a new country
met my future spouse outside a poet's door—
the poet who had already written
of *The Right Madness on Skye*

which year and when the confusions of biography
him and me outside that door
my future Grandma and Grandpa
leaning on the railing of their passage
this is me on the motorway
passing Grandma's Kilmarnock
and not stopping—
there in Grandpa's Glasgow
not stopping to see 3 St Ronan's
me passing mother's father's New Lanark
never once stopping in the Perth
of my ancestor Grahams—

my share of Scotland
now sunk in the bones of this house around me
full of cats and dust and lavender air
the occasional salty wrench of seaweed
travelling the mile in from low tide

do I thank my ancestors mourn St Ronan's
the road not taken the stone unturned
into life unknown

my grandparents chatting not yet matched
as they look out to their New my Old World
as we both cross difficult waters
all that and more who I'm not—
ploughing ahead passing each wave
not stopping never once stopping

How To Explore The Land of Your Ancestors

—for Jocelyn, family genealogist—

1. Wear your fingerprints, embrace your DNA
2. Have a cold (Heraclitus says a dry soul is wisest
   and best but Heraclitus undoubtedly
   never travelled Scotland
3. You must expect to be somewhat damp here
4. —This isn't Greece after all)
5. The cold will numb you
   so you don't quite notice
6. When you're overwhelmed
7. And it will help you parse strong accents
8. And besides you like to feel
   a little viral wherever you go
9. But carry lots of tissue
10. And extra patience to offer those
    who sleepless against your battering
    cough are
11. In need of rest
12. Are unnerved by
    your almost effortless switch
    to the road's left side
13. Drive carefully drive yourself carefully
    drive others with the greatest of care
14. Forget where you are
15. Fall in love with stone and forget about trees
16. They're grown in regiments here anyway
17. Fall in love with grey stone sky water
18. And the greenest of green hills
19. Spend days staring at the stones of castles
20. Of brochs
21. Of abbeys
22. Of cairns
23. And lining underground caverns
24. And those standing

25. In rows and circles
26. Don't snub the fallen
27. Spend days admiring stone on beaches
28. Laugh at the lamb's antics
    in the fields
29. Eat them
30. Love the rain pinging against your face
    or rising as mist around you
31. Love the lochs
    those salted those fresh
32. Decide that even as a Statement
    kilts are best not worn
    with rugby shirts
33. But are fine on road workers
    near Fort William
34. Be happy when your landlady is named
    for a goddess
35. Choose a nettled cottage
    tumbled
    as your own
36. Find where stories were surely told
37. Where the faery queen carried off
    Thomas the Rhymer
38. The crossroads where Tam Lin
    shivered naked in Janet's arms
39. Where Bonnie Charlie went from win
    to defeat to defeat
40. Find the land where clan warred and starved
    and killed for cattle
41. Learn to read gravestones
    to find the humour in the hourglasses
    the skull & bones
    humble praises lauding phrases dire warnings
    simple ends
42. Find your fingerprints (grubby and virulent)
    everywhere

Postcards From The Edinburgh Fringe

oh, you knucklenut yells a cabbie to jaywalkers
oh, you foolish virgins

howl howl howl howl howl
Cordelia is the fool guiding
a raw and tender Lear

beleaguered Lady Macbeth
agonizes over a British Home Stores bag
full of sound & fury

locals walk invisibly home
like Pictish Stones under wraps in a gallery
a brass band blares behind them
shrill bagpipes and jazz knotting before

children hiss at the lions
at the end of railings

silver Mayan chiming balls ring
faery change into pockets

Rosalind hides behind trees behind people
behind trees that are people
the look in their eyes at *run run Orlando;*
carve on every tree

there's every kind of kilted Scotsman

a formal white-shirted consort full
a bare-chested running youth
a grizzled-red bearded coot

when a dark-eyed punk glowers
and grins above his tartan
a band sporting Hawai'ian shirts
above theirs in chorus yells

Deep in the Heart of Texas

Oy

Aged Black, Morning Green: Edinburgh

ever-shifting leaf-filtered light
black branches gnarled dark as centuries
(soot on sandstone) islands of green
yet close to where lives piled high
in the tenements of the Royal Mile
paralleled rail-lines in a hollow once lake

height shifts everywhere we climb
through the post-tenement tourist mill
into St. Giles' Thistle chapel
we almost fall inside (its warm wooden
nest) spend hours lining our sights
to catch the beasts cavorting there

fish & chips brown sauce we eat
whatever's cheap in a park on stone steps
from bags smuggled into our room
(we carry spoons and a knife)
battered sausage meat pies
more fish more chips a gooseberry fool

Edinburgh's Antiquarian Bookshops guides us
the old pages dry our fingertips
dust our noses make our bags so heavy
(*no one* has the *Carmina Gadelica*)
we return to unload at our B&B before
we prowl more paper-powdered aisles

at night we walk as streets go quiet
climb Calton Hill pass the younglings
(nothing for us there) the crowds
come out from *Trainspotting* chat laugh
elbow the sophisticate theatrical turn
into smoky pub-light

we return to our room count our
treasures' pages (spoon a fool)
in morning light an artist chalks
the sidewalk swirling colour
while black dust in the wind devils
his corner (peppers my face)

we explore the small dead-ends of closes
varied light on varied stone the store
and house above called Gladstone's Land
(its kitchen a heart a hearth) its bedroom's
painted ceiling repeats between steady beams
flower fruit white bloom flash of red of green

Inchcolm Abbey

First trip past city
limits, out beyond
Edinburgh's skirts
and fields. First ferried
look at the Firth stark

blue, Inchcolm's stone and
green. Solid abbey
symmetry of walls
and a bell tower
I climb to see spread

out below my first
taste of the wonder
of ruins, all dark
narrow stairways and
corners, pieces of

the medieval floor,
the dormitory
huge—with only one
warming fire. First time
I think into a

place: imagine me
imagining the
plain rows of chilly
monks, white, grey-skinned with
cold, bright with holy

fires. First time feeding
local spirits: the
white and grey gulls who
barking like banshees
dog the ferry home.

What I Mean When I Talk About Ruins

Read the signs: viewpoint
ahead. Ancient monument.
Tower or folly.

Stone my spine:
my foundation, my spark.
Fragmented walls speak

my story. Once whole
and gracious, inhabited,
inside me folk breathed

and bred. But now not
shelter. Open to all
weather. What I am

speaks of what was once
here. Warning: dangerous ruin.
Do not trespass.

Do not clamber. Mortar cracks
to dust. And
the walls do not exactly

fall. They live
in wreckage. Imagine lives.
Imagine me. A monument

to what hands can build,
overcome by battles,
by time. By ivy's weight,

the long agonies
of frost, of rain, all
that fissures walls. Take me:

awash with weather
vertebrae and weeds flourish,
a different glory.

The Walk She Takes: Smailholm Tower

Slow in the weight of the fog
on the rolling lands of the Merse—green, green
old hills—she hears the steps of ghost horses,
echoing hooves and rain.

In this distance where there is no distance
all horses are ghosts,
all wind the lament of the border widow,
she: *I took his body on my back*
    And whiles I gaed, and whiles I sat;
    I digged a grave and laid him in
    And happ'd him up with sod sae green.

Walking she traces the furrowed line
of a runrig—lines
that disappear underfoot. Lines
of cottage walls
leaning up against the laird's protection.
She can step right over the barmkin now, so little
of its height remains,

step in and out of strangers' lives: the old lord
who lost three brothers and a son at Flodden,
then the years after staggered by reivers
stealing first 600 cattle then 123 then 60 then 6,
100 prisoners taken then 4.

It's here she finds her man leaning against a wall
of this tower brittle-patched with memories
patterned with blood and fear rising above the earth
into fog woven with wraiths and lamentations

crumbling alone. She's walking the borders,
she's out ghosting. She's getting used to harm.

Lockerbie

the body knows
                    with a seasick lurch
the name of this town

the body knows
                    loss
how in just an instant the world shifts

refuses to retake its accustomed shape
the body knows
                    what it means to fall

how a place will never again be just a name
the body knows
                    the steely shiver

that settles in my spine
how the day's air is suddenly weighted, cold
grey clouds now leaden

the body knows
                    I can see the words
I wrote about passing this place

but those pages are unaccountably blank
how I know
                    my body remembers

emptiness staggers me,
                    the sky crowding down
fear and loss

                    wrenching the gut
again
and again and again

Hermitage

Solid, severe, deceptively named
this castle reeks of rotting souls,
red swords, border reivers,
feuds, reprisals, maidens
abducted on their wedding days
released the worse for wear
captives slowly starved.

The stones still speak of this.
Blood, they say, scattered bones,
hidden dealings, plots and fevers
men held with lances
under the river till drowned
an evil lord boiled
wrapped in sheets of lead.

Entering at their own risk
visitors scuttle away
repelled by force of rancid air,
the malaise of atmosphere,
scatter to the thin relief
of buses and cars.
I'm in here alone.

Breathe shallowly.
Keeping this place out best I can.
I look around the cruelty
of these grim and grimy walls.
They weigh on me. The other face
of my castle dreams of fey Scotland.
The border country. I'm crossing it now.

Westerly

Atlantic Pacific

Why do I leave my shore for another?
Look west over the Atlantic

toward the wrong coast to my home?
Everywhere waves pulse on rock and sand,

drag lost things—stones, shells—grinding
them finer and finer, relentless

as the way I yearn over them, beyond them,
where whitecaps edge out to the everything

and nothing that is open sea/horizon/sky.
You could say gulls and waves again.

Small shadowed birds racing
on the tide-emptied sand. Bad weather

and rain breaking into sun. Small
brave bright flowers clinging to soil

no—creating the soil. If you dared
and I dare. I dare the black dog

to rise out of my bones, out of the shadows
to flicker fey at the edge of my vision.

Offer a vision. Mine/yours/another's.
Driving along the winding coastline,

marking the bends of the sea
as it shapes the land, I mark out

the threads of my life—
of a thousand other lives over time—

looking out over any ocean
I fall into myself; I fall away.

Westron Wind

My blood is half cedar. Half rain. Half the diffuse
northwestern light that pierces dense forest right
into me. Half the constant lap of waves on shore;
half their squall-chased roaring. Here, too,
Hebridean rain lashes rock grey sea—the whole
world smells of seawrack torn on the tide.
Westron wind blows. I have let go your hand,
turned to a landscape without trees, sure
it couldn't be lovely. Couldn't be loved.
Scotland was a faeryland, no fiery, no a tale told
by the embers I now walk among. Each step.
Each breath. Each stone under my shoe.
Each dire piece of what's ugly and beautiful,
history, I leave you behind because I love you.
I'm here to live my own middle ages, and
the small rain so busily rains down. My tales
mossed over, their bones in cairns, ivy
bringing their towers down stone by stone.
A streetscape etched with hunger, warpaths
worn smooth into lying peace. Sleep now,
love. I leave my life behind to come here. Alive
to this land, the sound of its rain, drenched
in its voices I read and imagine. Christ,
that my love were in my arms. The dross
left after the battle passes. It's in my bones.
I understand it all now: wind and rain
and raiders. I live it. Losing myself.
My blood is half raider. Half pain. Half the opaque
weapons one human will use against another
to hold lives in one hand for gain. Half
the constant need for vengeance; half
the peat fire's peace. And I in my bed again.
Crofts and clearances, O pioneers, it's all

stolen land. All grey sky full of rain torn awake
by shafts of breaking light. I'm lost
in fog lost here lost lost lost. I know I know I *know.*

1773

—stolen from Samuel Johnson's
A Journey to the Western Isles of Scotland—

January: Captain Cook
the first to cross the Antarctic Circle
March: Oliver Goldsmith, *She Stoops to Conquer*
December: The Boston Tea Party

August through October:
Samuel Johnson and James Boswell
make their tour of the Hebrides:

Of these Islands it must be confessed,
that they have not many allurements,
but to the mere lover of naked nature.
The inhabitants are thin,
provisions are scarce,
and desolation and penury give little pleasure.

The consequence of a bad season is here
not scarcity, but emptiness; and they
whose plenty, was barely
a supply of natural and present need,
when that slender stock fails,
must perish with hunger.

There is in the Island one house more, and only one,
that has a chimney: we entered it,
and found it neither wanting repair nor inhabitants;
but to the farmers, who now possess it,
the chimney is of no great value;
for their fire was made on the floor,
in the middle of the room,
and notwithstanding the dignity of their mansion,

they rejoiced, like their neighbours,
in the comforts of smoke.

The night came on
while we had yet a great part of the way to go,
though not so dark, but that we could discern
the cataracts which poured down the hills, on one side,
and fell into one general channel
that ran with great violence on the other.
The wind was loud, the rain was heavy,

and the whistling of the blast,
the fall of the shower,
the rush of the cataracts,
and the roar of the torrent,
made a nobler chorus of the rough musick of nature
than it had ever been my chance to hear before.

Whatever enlarges hope, will exalt courage;
after having seen the deaf taught arithmetick,
who would be afraid to cultivate the Hebrides?

Traigh Gheiraha Beach

a tropic-sea dream
deserted   but for
wind-ragged sheep on
grass-feathered dunes   its
pearly sand   dreamy

azure waves bitter-
cold   rough seastacks bite
austere northern sky
we wade through a storm-
carved tooth   treasure-hunt

on the strand: find snails
mussels   a sheep leg
& rib cage   gull wings
puffin skull   chill gnaws
our sun-beguiled skin

Giants Graves Forest Trail[1] Painted By Numbers

265[2,3] stairs through the forest[4]:
cross the stream[5] (small leap) step up up up[6]
to view Holy Island to view the beach[7]
2 saplings arch keystoneless across the path[8]
mossy stones in a clearing are the Giants Graves[9]
knee high waist high chest high
high above my head[10]
white buried in green, washed in it[11]
dusk surrounds on this constellation
of moons[12] its lines
of tall and fallen roofless guards[13]
nearby 1 tumbled shed[14] where:
1 tree veils a hole in the roof
1 small window
1 corner where the timeless rocks
have given up their work and sag[15,16]

---

1   Described in *Isle of Arran Forest Walks*.
2   I didn't count them.
3   My journal says "285" but given 2 above
    I go with authority cited in 1 above.
4   The forest was planted but I didn't mind.
5   Never noted.
6   Deeply noted.
7   We were duly warned
    we'd be able to do this. So noted.
8   Not described in any guidebook
    but journal-noted in an ironic tone
    (a less ironically noted frisson
    passing under them).

9   Ha! Of course they're not
    they're a cairn's remains duly fallen
    and buried in thick-heathered grass.
10 Roughly 5'4".
11 See 9 above.
12 Not literal moons
13 Or guides
14 Noted in no guidebook.
15 See 12 above. And the latter part of 9.
16 Note frisson. Note the sun setting.

Machrie Moor

A whole moor full of stones flies in the mist.
I'm alone and happy. It's the right time—

three groups leaving and a German couple
quickly here and gone. I went first to the Moss Farm

circles. I'd forgotten the strange almost
crystallized bits in the stones there. Then through

the Farm itself, taking some photographs
(scaring some sheep) and next to open moor

to the isolated tall stone. My pebble
from the Welsh standing stones visited there,

lying for some moments in a notch then rescued
safely back into my hand.

Also found someone's sage in a hollow.
Its scent unpretentious as the salty wind

from Machrie Bay. Then the three big stones,
a triad of giants whose aspect I try to absorb—

                                    —Afterward
I sat on the millstone to eat my honey ham

& coleslaw sandwich. Still sitting here. It's windy
and the sun comes and goes. Someone else arrives.

The wind sounds in the grass. Distant birds,
sheep, very distant cars—

                              —now I sit deep
in the bracken, waiting for more people to leave

and ducking out of the wind a bit (it's the kind
of sun and mist that creeps onto numbing flesh

like a crackling ice, thin and melting but sharp
and cold). It's warmer here. From my hollow

I can see the high circle prodding the light,
as the four-stone circle lowers into the ground

like numb beasts, and the lone stone,
and the trio, and the bump of the circle

I haven't been to yet. I love being here,
but it chills me—

                    —It's going to warm up now.
I sit in the second but farthest low circle

and the wind's rising. This circle feels so solid
and inside it is a certain *space* that opens.

I think the farthest ring with its small grey stones
is the most humble, the trio the most wizardly

the solo most heroic—circle on circle on circle—
the whole moor wheels spins lifts me into the mist—

Calanais

Celtic   Cross
3000   years
before   Christ
each stone time-
washed   wood
(knots   whorls
fractures) Lewis
stone   rises
solid   from
moorland's tides
& heather —a shape
like men   shoulders
inside   them
weary   weathered
once buried under 4 feet
of peat—   I make
3 clockwise circuits then 3
widdershins   pick a pebble a
cuckooflower—as I   circle   they shift weave
a tale between   themselves
they dance
while moon
swells & sighs
over
the hills:
the old
woman
of the
moors

Egg and Sky   Skye and Eigg

There's something about Skye
that reminds me   of Bogart
the way you can read history

in the lines on its skin
the Hebrides   rock-cold
with tales of blood and woe

layered   Stone   Bronze
all Ages Dark   laid bare by wind
that heartless moans across the moors

whistling up sea and sky
into storm to batter stone
steal feathers from birds   erode time

I walk through a castle ruin
in no one's care   a corner wall
stands high   windowed out

above a sheltered bay
but here   I'm no Bacall
or storied princess

even if I did wade through nettles
to reach that wall   that grinning
gap-toothed window is

the place I'm in   the Isle
of Skye   and more islands offshore
the places   I don't go now

since boats   and weather
time and tides   are hard to figure
and have been   for longer lifetimes

than I admit to   the places
offshore I long for
only smear the horizon

or shape appealing colours
on a map   off Skye there's
an island called *Egg*

Egg!   on my face   sunny-side up
or more like kestrels and gulls
cracking their anxious way

into the world   a puffin or three
I don't go there   do I
even think of it   do I   even look at it

from Skye's shore
leaning against this window
fingers abuzz   from nettle kisses

I recall Samuel Johnson saying
of Egg   *I have heard of nothing*
curious in it   but the cave

in which a former generation
of the Islanders were
smothered by Macleod

Egg shapes in my mind   the windswept
heathered slopes above
a folk cowering in a cave

farmers and shepherds
not warriors
and the entry blocked

by thuggish men in kilts
sealing out the air   later I check
a map for the name of

the castle I stand in
note I could have seen Egg
from there   or Eigg

as this guidebook's
map has it   the castle I thought
was Knock (the bay is) is named

Caisteal Camus   the bay *Cnoc Uaine*
where "one part with a window remains
to some height"   *yeah*

I've seen it   no mention of nettles
only that   in the 15th century
it was owned by Macleods

which chills me   Johnson's tale
overwrites the name Macleods
I see only   those who

would seal a cave   against the breath
of those inside
the castle's history

persists with tales of capture
of being   by Macleods   besieged
extended and remodeled   then

left abandoned
to decay   *beware*
the guidebook says   *of packs of dogs*

ah I say
me and Eigg both   kid
me   and Eigg both

On Skye

Hard to know the right madness here—
Skye's hills have the twisted pine scent
of Montana, the air of Coyote's

bitter-bright games—but this is where the road
crosses the bridge where Macleod
said goodbye to his faery wife

and leads to the ruins of Trumpan Church
where Clan Macdonald was burned alive
by Clan Macleod. The crofts crumple

like abandoned ranches, houses and barns
folding in on themselves, stones falling
one by one. Here it was not hard weather

that emptied the fields but the Clearances:
the landlords and everywhere their sheep.
Stacks and hills and emptiness. Stones

rearing to the sky: churches and brochs
bending stone by stone nearer the grasses,
castles full of nettles and sheep, weeds

growing right to the sea, and everywhere,
on church walls, sea rocks, corners
of the castle windows, a strange green fern,

bright with brownish stems, everywhere
springing from the cracks in stone.
I dreamt a dog whose hair was these

ferns, thick, rich, alive. Looking at her
I saw how the stones love this land,
how the rain and wind and tides love stone,

how the grass does, how the woman who
once lived in the fallen croft shaped scones
from flour and sang while her children—

who grew to leave for the New World—
woke to the sure rhythm of her work
and the haunting lilt of a piper's tune

reeling in the righteous wind.
All this, with my fingers woven into fronds
on the greened dog's back, moving from

the cool growth to the warmth that rose
from her skin. And in the pause of flying home,
right at the Rockies' feet, there she is again:

standing stiff in the wind as my plane
touches down on the runway right by her.
A coyote on the tarmac, the blowing snow

swirling around her feet like fog,
like the cold and deep warmth
of her feral, human breath.

Auchindrain

*A small farming village in the western Highlands,
Auchindrain is preserved as an open air museum. The
cumulative power of the buildings, spaces, and objects—and
the information they show in such sensory detail about the
villagers' day-to-day activities—makes exploring the site like
reading the community's history with all its echoes, a rare
window into the lived experience of ordinary folk and an
antidote to wars and raids and lairds and castles. A
textural archeology.*

Auchindrain Inventory: Village Museum

ragweed: *yellowish*
bramble: *yellow & grey*

these are the dyes & the colours they make

meadowsweet: *bright yellow   brown*
alder: *dark brown*

for the handspun wool hand-woven
into herringbone tweed

iris: *green & light brown*
tormentil: *whitish*
bog myrtle: *mud brown   orangish yellow*
heather: *dark orangish yellow   medium brown*

warm & weatherproof here in the grey damp

nettle: *yellowish cream   brownish grey*
greyish medium-to-dark brown
lichens: *white   pink   rich orangish brown*
reddish brown   bluish grey

the old breed of sheep smaller   more delicate
the wool fine   had to be housed in winter
not commercially successful
now extinct

*

Auchindrain = *Achadh an Droughinn*
= The Field of the Thorntree
its name first written in the 1470s

its use much older
settled by Scots from Ireland:
in whose language great poetry is still given voice

               *

township   farming village   cluster of cottages
lost in the hills   a Brigadoon
empty of lives but remnants
pictures   mementos
scraps of knowledge   fragments of tales

Eddie MaCallum was the last
farmed here until 1962
Eddie MaCallum was the last alone
here once six families decided
by lot the choice of arable land—
Eddie MaCallum the last   alone and last
Eddie MaCallum gone

a town standing witness to itself

               *

constant work to keep the village self-reliant
governed by seasons
seed-time & harvest   movement of stock
on & off the hill

planting bere & oats for their grain and straw
stacked on stone with a base of brushwood
matured then dismantled & the grain thrashed
to a drying kiln when threshed
to a hand quern to grind

keeping the sheep lambing and milking (mix
tar & ewe's butter   rub into the sheep's skin
to keep parasites at bay)

cattle   sheep   cockerel   hens   other fowl   pigs
that drovers took to market

dogs & cats

daily work: *sorting the beasts*
redding up = maintaining buildings   dykes   drains

*

house   cottage   byre   barn
one house with stone walls whitewashed
a chimney   thatch strapped down
chicks & hens a-scratch in the yard
cobbles by doors to keep out the mud

then the cottar's cottage: walls   roof   smoke hole:
smoke eventually found its way out
common entry to house & byre
the cottar given house & kailyard
for a time in return for work
grass thickens its loose thatch

the cottar smelling of smoke and damp
a season of work   sweat and sleep
dusted with harvest
chaff part of the weave of his clothes   wonders
what roof will cover him in the next winter's rains

does he have parents?
is he too poor   for wife and child?
does he bring them   leave them   where?

does anyone know the cottar's tale?
if the cottar had a daughter
would he name her Isabella?

*

dry stone pointed with clay mortar
all houses altered & rebuilt

buried in the walls are stumps
for cruck frames to hold the roofs
later replaced by wall-head couples & rafters
old doorways for people & beasts blocked
then new ones broken out of the stone

byres changed to stables   peat stoves to cart sheds

loft or part lofts   some with attics
floors a recent thing   older places closet   kitchen
byre under one roof   closet for butter
& cheese making   removed from byre
a kitchen to cook & eat in   & where most slept

*

Dan MacDonald   apprenticed as mason
to Stoner Munro   Dan MacDonald
(Dangerous Dan? Dastardly Dan? Dan Dead-Shot?)
could sit in bed at one end of the loft
& shoot rats around the meal kists at the other

That's all we're told of Dan (Stoner Dan?
Dan the Mason? Rat-Killer Dan?)

*

houses built end on to the wind
dark   smoky: *clarty but cosy*

women spun by the fire   the most social place
kitchens first open hearths
then fireplaces with back-stone
added hoods to carry smoke up
finally internal stone gable & flue
at *best* end of house

*

barns built across the prevailing wind:
2 doors set opposite
for the through draft to blow away chaff
 while winnowing

*

over the whole site flowers & herbs
once bound in gardens spread freely

water carried from springs
cattle in the byre end
barrel sunk outside door for liquid manure
to fertilize kailyard or mordant for dying wool
a *knee of timber* helped to keep a barrow-load
or 2 of turnips by the door
salt tub for pickling meat

heather thatch on a layer of rushes
with layer of turf beneath
lying on a birch frame

peat store   pigsty   hen house   cart storage

kailyard walled to keep out beasts:
kail   parsley for broth   turnips   a few potatoes
red currants   blackcurrants   gooseberries
mint   tansy   a Pyrennena lily

too boggy around the burn for sown crops
but here some grazing   some meadow hay
2 kinds of rushes:
the jointed which cattle will eat
the common rush which they won't
used for thatching
& the pith for wicks for burning oil in cruisies

meadowsweet   valerian   red clover   flag iris
willow planted for baskets & rope

rowan trees—berries for jelly
but as much encouraged
for protection from witches

                          *

a ferryman at Inverary used
to visit an old lady who lived in Auchindrain
now a ruin   *her house was black*
—nothing but a cruisie—
and the scones were black, and she was black, too
children thought she was a witch

in her garden: selfheal   feverfew
sneezewort   woundwort
yarrow = *Luschosgadh na fola*
= herb of the staunching of the blood

46

in the smoke of her house   herbs hang
drying in smoke
scones on the griddle poised above the fire
she was black, too

*

proteins: milk   cheese   fish   oatmeal
potatoes   occasionally salt meat
carbs: oatmeal   barley   meal   potatoes
fats (never enough):   butter   the little meat
vitamins & minerals from these & vegetables
honey ale & soft fruits were the sweets
eggs only in spring—poultry eaten only
on special occasions

coalfish & pollack caught off rocks
in summer by the young
split   salted   dried

flounders speared in shallows
cod & haddock caught in long-lines in deepest water
herring in Loch Fyne famous
several men would work at it in summer
trout from burns & hill lochs:
river trout   sea-trout   salmon

a sheepskin buoy atop the nets

*

Light = often just firelight
cruisies burned fish oil
a rush dip for special reading   writing letters
(a stalk of common rush   soaked in melted tallow
after being peeled   lasted 8–10 minutes)

The well-off houses would make tallow candles
and later own a paraffin lamp

Soap homemade from ashes & tallow
Washing outside

Inside the house until 1760–1860
just a chest & some stools
after that dresser commonplace
1800s decorative chinaware
wall-clocks a status symbol

willow creel   elderwood netting needle
hazel crook   heather rope
heather twigs gathered with twine for potscourer
birch besom

baking stone for oatcakes & barley bannocks

Usually the only iron ware in house
was a 3-legged pot   after 1750 cast iron
before riveted metal plates
(it was often the only cooking vessel)
then later a kettle & griddle
spoons of horn
masher from wood   horn mug

riddle with groats for grinings
quern—handmill for oat & barley meal

bellows for peat fire
heather whisk for ashes

*

the kind of industry   few of us know
small routines of the daily beasts
larger cycles of planting, reaping, birthing

long summer days to manage the crops to shore up
the walls before the long wet winter darkness

a child learns to feed the beasts   to milk to plant
to harvest   to love   to marry   to bury

*

willow for
    wattling   creels   baskets   bindings   medicine
rushes for
    thatch   lamp wicks
    beasts' bedding   occasionally grazing
ash for
    plough   tools   carts   boats   machinery
eldge (now scarce) for
    netting needles   shuttles   musical instruments
    toys   small tools   wines   medicines
birch twigs make superb brooms
    stain-resistant wood for dairy utensils
    bark for tanning leather
hazel for
    shepherds' crooks   fishing   thatching rods
    creel   basket frames
heather for
    thatch   strong rope   dye   basket & creel
    brooms   pot-scourers   hard-weather grazing

oak for
  fuel for iron smelting
  shipbuilding   heavy construction

                  *

piper & singers   then fiddler
most every house had a trump (mouth harp)
or later a *mootheir* (mouth organ)
Box melodeon

tunes & songs reeling out   into long nights

                  *

in the traditional long-house = byre dwelling:
  byre
  Bridal chest plain
  Kitchen:
    2 boxbeds   linen chest   drawer in bottom
  closet/milkhouse
  parlour
    hand-embroidery with Celtic designs
    feathers in jar   family pictures
    cradle   humble china cupboard
    iron bed   chest   2 prints
    rug   rocker   chair   good fireplace

                  *

caschrom = foot plough
operator works backwards   efficient & effortless
1 acre = 70 hours

50

*

Isabella   Bell Pol   Muddy Bell
at the end of her life
came back to live out her days here
because giving her a house
exempted the town from the parish poor rate

Isabella   Bell Pol   Muddy Bell
unmarried daughter of a cottar
kept house for her father till he died
then she laboured in the lead mines
till she had to retire

Isabella   Bell Pol   Muddy Bell
her tidy house a stack of peat   a fireplace to cook in
boxbed walled & curtained
to keep night's warmth in old bones
a kettle   a pot   a griddle   a cruisie
a rush basket   a wool throw
a table   a bench   a chair   a stool   a dresser
a horn spoon   some china   a mirror

who left the eggs on the dresser for you
Isabella   Bell Pol   Muddy Bell

*

a weaver was one of the few
who lived by practicing a trade

    bracken: soft/light/medium brown
    indigo

    clover: soft light medium brown
    poppy leaves: soft grey

dandelion: soft light orange
onion skin: soft light brown
blueberry: dark brown
thistle: soft grey
St. John's wort: light light beige
foxglove: dark cream
wild daisies: soft brown

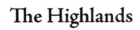

The Highlands

By Road By Ruin

The sheep a scatter of white
below the green mountain. The empty road.
Grey wind on the hills—that wind
shears the sheep as well as any clippers.

That wind tears the shawl from my hands.

But back to the sheep. Some walk on.
Some lean against fences chewing pale grass.
This land has stone enough to make anyone
build a castle—there's another:
a pile of crumbling stones
on the next hill above the ford
where sheep cross like a twist of pebbles
drifting from a builder's hand.

The names of the fields are as old
as the mud that fills them.
Ivy and nettle tangle the ruins.

My hands sap-stained, my legs stung.

I climb to look out over another wall
to find a further green ditch bothered by sheep,
by stone, by the wake of the builders,
clans and the victors of battles. Rampagers,
berserkers and their wives.
The crofters tending gentle sheep
and their wives.

Evicted. Evicted for more sheep.

All is layered here with the tumult of weather
the generations who have lined the road
with stone walls, velvet fields, rubble.

I walk them, current snaking my hair.

My head full of stories, castles,
ruin and rain, the lives of the women
who built and bred and baked
and died and whose daughters live.

Each stone is a pillow for someone's sleep,
for fallen walls and twigs dust-deviled
by the mountainous turbulent wind
that combs through the Seven Sisters: peaks
lit by cloud-shifting wind
against skies blackened by rain.

In the rain still the same sheep in the hollows;
I'm placid as sheep here. Wind shears me.

What can I do
but walk on into the ancient weather?

Graves and Churchyards Cairns and Cairns

a pantoum

By whom the subterraneous vaults are peopled is now utterly unknown. The graves are very numerous, and some of them undoubtedly contain the remains of men, who did not expect to be so soon forgotten.

—Samuel Johnson,
A Journey to the Western Isles of Scotland

the afterlife alive under stone
peopled by shadows skulls unruly dust
we're time-travellers in a world of bone
tourists in cairns souterrains tombs

peopled by shadows skulls unruly dust
and remnants of eagles deer and dogs
tourists in cairns souterrains tombs
from an age when giants were known to roam

and remnants of eagles deer and dogs
add fleetness to the weight of human remains
from an age when giants were known to roam
they sleep now in mounds and under church floors

add fleetness to the weight of human remains
let walls rise over them blocks of stone
they sleep now in mounds and under church floors
speak from the ground beneath our feet

let walls rise over them blocks of stone
each fragment placed by human hands
speaks from the ground beneath our feet
how thin the flesh that nets our bones

each fragment placed by human hands
we are the gravid robbers of graves

how thin the flesh that nets our bones
we belong here by our presence alone

we are the gravid robbers of graves
we're time-travellers in a world of bone
we belong here by our presence alone
the afterlife alive under stone

Kilmichael Glassary

near the school house
on a small rise
up the valley's side
a place where such things
are carved and schools built
Bronze Age cups
hollowed as by water
and rings some pattern
some design *carved*
by whose hand whose eye
to what purpose
on a natural rock outcrop
in the grass a bed of grey stone
transversed by faults like wood grain
the 150 carvings on this rock
cup cup cup and ring
cup encircled by ring
two cups yoked by a ring
where the eye wants to create a beast
a series of lines
their purpose unknown
speaking of delight in ornament
boasting of war
marking presence or grief
writing I was here I was here I was
they map absence now
some are overgrown by moss
some fill with dried grass
some with rain

Poltalloch O'Clock

Tell me the time. The time
is Botallack o'clock.
This is the dead of night.
      —W.S. Graham,
   "Lines on Roger Hilton's Watch"

what time it is:
  Skipness Castle
  St. Brendan Chapel
  Clainaig: a grouse dust-bathing in a ramp
  townly gull-pressed seaside Tarbert
  Castle Sween twice unseen
  Benfield Bay's stuttering breeze

but surely:
  Dunadd hillfort: with the Stone of Destiny
  marked with Ogham words, a footprint, a bowl,
  the weathered boar engraved,
  edges of wall, grass,
  a bit of blown wool

still perhaps:
  Kilmartin's linear cemetery:
  a line of cairns down the glen
  North Cairn (Megalithic)
  Mid Cairn (Bronze Age)
  South Cairn
  great heaps of stones
  axes etched in rock

yet again:
  Temple Wood's stone circle
  and cyst grave (swirl-carved stone)
  Ri Cruin circle

(axe markings like pennants on stone)
(one tall stone fenced off in a field)

else:

Kilmartin Church
with its Celtic crosses
outside Poltalloch gravestones line up
the crossbones the skull and Latin
the crests the knights and

now:

Poltalloch stones, what time are we?
It's ever it's always
Poltalloch o'clock

Carnasserie Castle

God be with O Duibhne inscribed in Gaelic
over the door, the dressed stonework here

refined, well-displayed by the corbelling,
string-courses, moulded frames and panel

carving, all in the latest fashion—in 1572.
And by the Gaelic is the builders' armorial,

together with royal arms that record his
marriage to Jean, the king's natural daughter.

Just a hundred years later this work blown up
during a rebellion against the king. A hundred

years a home, then a ruin, Carnasserie banks
its remains on the ridge above Kilmartin Glen:

above Dunadd the Bronze Age hillfort, above
the ley line of Stone Age cairns, standing stones,

patterning a dance our feet cannot remember,
the stone face marked in cups and rings telling

a tale we'll never know, above all these, four-square,
weathered, battered, the castle walls still proclaim

a new age of fashioned stone brought down.
My father's camera eye catches: the grey stone

carved in long, still-perfect strands around
corbelled corners; the grace of the two square

towers and the wall drawn web-taut between;
the Gaelic words and carved arms, proclaim

proud connections; the plastic-sealed plaque
describing the castle in the fewest words it can;

me resting out on the ledge behind a steel-gridded
lower window; Mom and I sentinals at the top

of the castle's rail-guarded watch, staring out
over the valley's layers of time, thinking how

all our known history is a blink of time's eye
a camera shutter snapping to hold the little

we can know, a remnant of time's fashion
in a language nearly lost. How much it

meant to the living then, how little now.
And yet it stands and means, shines

forward out of the moment's *fashioning*.

Hunting the Lady Well:
Near Rosemarkie, The Black Isle

a sestina

Fence-caught goat rescued, we leave; the gate
shut behind us, round the tricky-rocked point.
I choose the beach route, confidently navigate sea-
brown sand—but instantly flounder thigh-deep.
Chastened, mud-limned, I clamber back
to my parents' solid ground, rejoin our search.

Mom takes high, Dad low, I the middle, we search
the wooded hill like a sieve, a fence, a gate
wide open, between us everything escapes back
into the hidden world. We quickly reach a point
too far, turn to retrace our steps: somewhere deep
in the green-burdened woods above the sea

the well is guarded by undergrowth dark as sea's
bottom. The forest-maze daunts us, still we search.
Through whips of brush and branches, we're deep
in shade, each space between tree trunks a gate
into shadows—striding through, we're drifting points
aware in the murky air, as though wandering back

in time, in place, in memory. My parents far back
behind me now, I orient by the cough of the sea;
waves lurch loud on the bay between rocky points
while above me leaf-rattle masks my search.
I can't find the centre, the other world, the gate
muffled in layers of forest so thick and rain-deep

I taste a weed-chocked wilderness so deep
it locks my throat. I know the well is here, back
in ground I keep crossing, my mud-spattered gait
awkward, anxious, sad. Pause. Listen: above the sea

and its rush threads a watery sound not wind. Search
the sudden stillness. A bush tied with rags points

to water, glass-clear. A waist-high stone the point
water breaks into a pool of wonder, mystery deep
in filtered light, not a place for anxious search
but to listen, to find. It's real, not somewhere back
in time, in museums. Splash my face, sluice off sea
muck. Water hazes, clears. I tie a rag: a gate

for me into this place's deep liquid heart, a gate
that points to all returns, spilling from hill to sea.
I call my still-searching parents; it calls me back.

Kilchurn Castle Picturesque

Rough waters: steel-blue, white-capped
like the clouds above. Low hills raise the sky,
shade up to hunter green, sage green,
then misty mountain blue. A storybook view
across the loch to where Kilchurn nestles at its edge
etched out against the loch like a hill itself.
Closer, and towers define themselves,
windows yaw and gape,
chimneys dagger a path to the sky.

Above the doorway: 1693 and crowns. A shield.
Ropes twined like snakes and Celtic knottery.
We climb and duck. I pose,
surprised in an archway. A fallen turret
the plinth for a statue my now-dead father becomes,
my mother laughing at us, she who now
has forgotten her life. In my camera Kilchurn's light
sears this instant into history, true beauty:
grey stone and a span of grace.

The Grey Cairns of Camster

I stand inside one of the chambers
of the long cairn, drenched, hesitant
in my black raincoat, my long greying hair

plastered on head and coat. Paper
and pen in hand, I know that
I don't quite fit, that I am nowhere

near able to lose myself here.
It's my penchant for graveyards
that brings me here, for stone,

and for places named Grey
with narrow passages that sometimes
I'll wade on my knees through mud

and 5000 years for. The rolling hillside,
the stone piled on it casually, as though
simply tilled from the fields. People lived

and died on this land, and inside these cairns
they placed their dead. Generations later
they sealed the mounds and left them,

deliberately, as though packing to move on,
closing the cottage for winter.
Now archeologists have come and gone,

cleared the place of flint tools, pottery,
charred human bones. Imagine
the dead, their burnt bones, tools laid by

for future use or to commemorate
what was made. Pottery holding what—
food? grain? emptiness?

You must imagine this
—the dead and their memories
and their future heaven. Picture me

in the midst of their dim light,
standing stones holding more stones up
long centuries. How the camera flash

fills the room between me and my father,
how the ghosts flee before it.
Then to the Grey Cairns of Camster—

three tombs. One round one to the left,
and two in the other set—horned platforms outside.
Couldn't get in the round one (too muddy)

or one of the long ones, because the passage
was too long and a little difficult.
Crawled into the other, skylight. Poured rain.

Sinclair and Girnigoe Castles

here's one of the ways   a castle may still stand
padlocked signposted   but danger is me

camera-armed taking   no prisoners striding past
the sign edged by wind   and riotous sea

there a tumult of sun   crowns castle within castle
the bright-dark sky   suffers predations of birds

and steady invasions   of waves scouring tales away
one remains: legend says   that in 1571 the 4th Earl

dungeoned his son and heir   seven years that
he fed him salted beef   so he died mad with thirst

one wall from salty sea   so hard to tell where
eroded layers of sand-   stone end and eroded

stonework begins   one of the ways a castle
may fall into Sinclair Bay   I keep my eyes open

spend days getting   to know this castle's
winds the constant pass   of sun and cloud

the Sinclairs tell me   the thirsty son
died elsewhere later   having suffered only

as much of a salted   beef winter as everyone did
they have plans to rebuild   the castle or at least

shore the ruins against   the tides of time and
history and visitors   like me who want

to touch everything   to think they know
something of this toppling   history not their own

to be of these castles   of the majestic ever-changing
sky and lurking shadow   a moment's owner

a moment's keeper   land-holder
keeper of trust   a moment's lord

Duncansby Stacks, Caithness

Down onto the flattened grass
   onto the stark wire of fences
along the spines of steel posts: rain.
   I've slowed, hiking, dawdled into
my own time alone away from the roils
   of this millennium's continually
boiling sour news; its noise fades
   into distant chatter; sea wind
scrubs my face, scours the dirt path
   clean. I could put those
two words together: rain and wind
   and come up with torrent
or the mist that veils all
   from cloud to sea. I could.
Or count the men and boats not here
   the herring gone. They're not
of this time, places like this
   where fewer live now than in
centuries past. So I can name nothing.
   Instead I lumber forward,
keeping watch for signs of fools
   out like me: Vikings cursing
the weather, or blue-dyed
   Picts in the folds of land ready
to battle them. Wisely, there's
   not even a sheep out here.
The loudest sounds, the largest beings
   are liquid and the air throwing
it around. Even in me, pneumonia
   wheezing in my lungs, kicked up
by walking and by weather.
   I clear the hill: ranging before me
the sea, these sea stacks
   haystack-shaped and twinned.

They could almost be a store of winter
    feed, a hut, a howe, a dovecote.
Except how the waves blow into them.
    How I cough and stare at them.
How the gulls ride the grey slide
    of rain to them. How they are claimed
by the tides and mist. What time
    is this? What century? Which
conquering tribe threatens to ravage
    the people and land? The rain and wind
batter me: wash out my moorings
    faster than fever can dry my face,
the rain, the windy light, as time
    falls through me. What race am I being
born into? What time am I now?
    My black jacket whips like a flag
from no country, tethered by my body's
    weight, my feet my anchor against
the incoming weather. It is the rain season
    in the year of wind, and rocks ahead
dressed like shore. It's a wild world
    we're riding in a storm we can only
hope is cleansing. Batten down.
    Batten down.

The Orcadian Saga

Walking The Land's Edge

History cannot ignore genetics. It is a record of our origins. Our past is a combination of culture and biology. One without the other is only half the story.

—Sir Walter Bodmer

The shore is stepped
            with layers of sandstone,
raddled with tide-wrack, rich in the sun.
                  We clamber
up the ledges across the stone plains
                bloodred,
lava black, the tan of our skins.
              The hill's green
just ends, breaks into this wealth of stone
tumbles down
          as though falling here
is what must be done.
            We jump from edge
to edge where the ledges march out
to the sea. Such stones

made the Ring of Brodgar
and slates
       for the sea-town's streets.
Their dull clatter is a sound
we want to live by,
  but here the rush of waves says
              hush
listen: this is what you're made of.
              Blood's shush
and patient centuries. This is what
eternity does:
       pushes us forward and back
against the shore. Says look:
          here a line

undulates like vertebrae,
the earth's back
                    slipping into the waves
and gone, then tide-change
and
      it leaps and dives
and curls and dips and rises
                         like fish
from under the waves.

The Scrawlings: Maes Howe

each winter for
5000 years the sun

marks solstice on the back walls   even the Vikings

sought this treasure
breaking in finding

nothing but bones   inscribing their boasts

these runes
were carved by the man

most skilled in runes in the western world

I carved this dragon
made this cross

Ingigerth is the most beautiful of women

(beside it is etched
a slavering dog)

Thorni bedded   Helgi carved   Ingebjorg the fair widow

we have been here
we have *seen*

I come here under the barrow

Tomb of the Eagles

—for Ronald and Morgan Simison—

I'm left-handed like her—the child
who made this shard, who shaping a pot
marked its rim with her thumbnail,

the etch etch etch of her hand on red clay
then the vessel shattered with her grandparents'
clean bones, and with her own. Her knife fits

my fingers. She carried it close;
her hands fit where my fingers rub
the notched edge.

Morgan Simison's palms slide over
5000 years of burial,
her hands trace the furrow where

the skull bowed under the slow press of a strap
slung with the weight of fuel, food, child.
A life of hard work for a simple meal.

But among the bones no sign of violence—
survival enough toil for them all.
The blunt affection of her hands on the bone.

She loves what she knows of these long dead,
who worked the lands her family tills. The tomb
her husband uncovered built by generations

of hands that knew these cliffs, this soil.
The stories we can't guess, why the bones
of sea-eagles mix with their dead.

I want to shape the child's name, whatever words
she had for *bowl* and *knife* and *the ragged sea*
below the cliffs of her tribe's tomb,

the seal swimming alone among the rocks,
whatever words she would use for the way
my thumb fits into the prints left by her own.

Dwarfie Stane, Isle of Hoy

A tomb cut into a rock, rare
and rectangular on the bench
below the bouldered mountain,
on green and purple heather
bright on the peat.
White in the promise of sun,
it's named for the local belief
that a dwarf made a home here—
and he or someone surely did,
carved an entrance to a bed
and a place to store what was needed
for someone's sleep.

I crawl in,
turn awkwardly and sit—the cold
runs through my body. And I hum.
Some power there left by the hands
that shaped the careful bed,
the chambered ledges, the rim
above the door, squeezes song
from me, wordless, half voice
half vibration, the echo so close
it's my own voice beside me.

It's white in there, white
with shadow, with someone's
long sleep, with some kind
of dream like the hum of wind
in the carved walls embracing
a dwarvish residence, a presence
in that small emptiness
humming the broken song beside me
in a language of hollowed stone.

Westness Walk: Rousay

When a mile-long walk can take you 5000 years
(from farm to grave, a miracle of geography,

of transdimensional space) how can you believe
this is simply a beach? On a small island?

In the far north, north of Scotland, north
of the civilized world? It is. Low waves shadow

your steps, echo them, count you as one
of the passing fray. They don't mind you one bit.

So you start at the beginning, at Midhowe,
where the humble rusting hangar shelters

the stalled, empty graves of Neolithic farmers.
You're on a walkway above them. What do you

look down on? All of those 5000 years,
or more? Each stall marks where the bones

now aren't. How can you imagine the hands
that made these? You can't. Step out

into the salt wind. On the promontory you trace
Midhowe broch. It's new: first century B.C.E.,

the Iron Age, is almost like home now, isn't it?
Isn't it? Okay, try Brough Farm which flourished

between 1200 and 1600, surely that's easier
and you've already come a few steps down the beach.

Another broch here. You try to imagine the towers
so close, how the people might have huddled there

against raiders, then spilled out in safety
across the fields. Still no easier. Damn.

How about the Wirk? What? Not enough left
to imagine at all. So St. Mary's Church.

Surely that's easier. The small shape buttressed
to keep it from sliding down the slope,

or better yet here's Skaill farm, empty since
The Clearances. The Norseness of its name

drags you to Viking times. Does that make you
uneasy? The dragon prows? The horned hats?

Walk on. Here's another stalled chambered tomb.
Knowe of Roweigar, safely buried in turf. The cow

by the notice board eyes you with something
like disdain. You pass the Knowe of Swandro

(a broch, again kindly buried, visible only
to the knowledgeable eye), the Norse Hall

(Vikings again). So here an uneventful walk
to Moa Ness, where Picts and Vikings buried

their dead. You are pleased to hear the Picts
had no grave-goods, were simply laid in their graves.

That seems simple and clean. Not so the Viking
grave there, revealing a woman and her newborn,

she, covered with grave-gifts, two oval brooches,
a silvergilt pin with gold filigree and amber inlaid.

Now it strikes you. Now you can imagine the grief
of one who'd lay her there, them there, picture him

and the shovels of shore dirt, picture that grief.
See one death (one life) amongst all of these.

You're safe now. Pass the Noust, a simple
boat house. That's nothing much. Come now

to the end: Westness House, the laird's seat.
It's only a big farm, a manor; there are stories

here, too, those you don't need to make up
for yourself (Bonnie Prince Charlie! India!

Pre-Raphaelites and all! The 19th C!) There, now.
You're done. Come so far and you're not even tired.

The Tattoos

below my right shoulder
out on the plump curve of my arm
is no dragon, not the one the Vikings carved
on the walls of Maes Howe, the one some call a lion,
a wolf, a hare, no upright head
craned towards its back
where something like steam arises
from something like a sword
or is it a tail?
no four square legs, the left front
tricked up like a horse's
gesturing, prancing not in pain or pride;
which marks are its face,
which wings, which tail?
is that a sword?
are we meant to see this dragon slain?
not mine, mine is never slain;
mine rises from my arm
in its stark lyrical lines,
the swoop of back to neck
throat to paw, and the sacred space defined
between that and the other the solid certain line
from chest and belly—and is that a wing?

I Don't Have

and not on my left ankle
just above the jutting bone
where calf begins to swell
isn't what was briefly hennaed
on the back of my hand
isn't the crescent and V-rod, no,
not the broken arrow superimposed
upon a curving piece of moon
someone thought it might be
a symbol of death or of man and
woman, who knows what
the wild Picts in
their woad-stained skins were
thinking, not me, but without the arrow
there is no point,
no curls of fletching, no V
to hold up everything in the world;
without the moon and its pelta patterns
curved to mark the craters
of its eyes, nothing tips everything
back down to the earth,
nothing bears me up, and
nothing, nothing holds me down

Petraphilia

Waves love stone. Watching, you feel like
a voyeur: their relation so personal, intimate,
ancient. It's a metaphor for marriage, storm and
calm, the changing tides, water shaping stones,
stone giving water a place to fall, to pool, to rise
to become cloud and fall again. Ancient. They
can take each other for granted. Or even granite.
Here's a story: outside grey-stony Stromness,
if you walk the beach west past Churchill's bunkers,
west toward the cemetery, you might start to see
how the stone of each small bay you walk
is a different colour of sunset: *amber umber smoke*
soot apricot plum soot peach storm. Then you glance
up to see a wall, each stone placed and known by
callused hands and beyond that the gravestones,
families' grief and pride channeled by the carver's
chisel. Above those, hills full of cairns, tombs,
howes, words for stones arranged around the bones
of our dead, keeping holy the fragile stones once
inside our flesh. The end. Listen to the waves. You'd
never guess they're slowly eating stone. Wind does
too but water is master here: *stone, I will love you*
till I wear you away. We'll be one then, I swear.
I might scour you to sand but will forget you never.
I'll break you. Undermine you. But will not forget. I will
never not touch you. I love your every curve and edge,
I kiss you lick you roar and bite. How can you not
believe the tale of the stone standing on the hill
who one day each year can bear it no more but must
walk down to the lake and drink? How could it not?
See its face in the water, stern and devoted. *Amber*
umber smoke apricot plum soot peach storm. The end.

Wearing Nothing But The Midnight Sun

—Summer Solstice—

History is traditionally blind
to these movements of ordinary people

because it is dominated by culture and artifacts
I read these words on
the shortest night of the year

in a place where the sky never darkens but dims

we've spent this day circling the 30 remaining
stones standing to shape the Ring of Brodgar

learning the time-washed year-carved edges

of each stone
I showed you the Viking graffiti

we followed how sun's line

pierced the haze breaking
on cloud-washed stone

grey, grey-green, golden and whorled

now it's night but the dimming sunlight still
pours into the attic room we're given to sleep in

a room dressed mostly in pink

ruffled wherever a ruffle could go
our hostess named Venus truly for real

it's our anniversary the small dusky hours of solstice

your mouth on my mouth
my hand slides down the

primitive terrain of your back

we ring and circle each other
our purpose ancient, lost to history

mysterious as stone

tonight ghost lovers
walk the Ring of Brodgar

learning the wear of each stone

while they lose themselves
in the silk of skin on earth on stone

and then on each other

tasting one another as we do
touch wakening the powers of the skin

the fingertip's whorls pressing

into the turf of each other's flesh
pulses beating in their ears

these movements of ordinary people

their cries like gulls
as lost in the instant they name each other

created anew by each other's fingers

bones and muscles lost to time
we name ourselves

Missing You In Stromness

Someday I'll show you
Logan's Well where ships watered

before the long crossing:
Captain Cook's *Resolution* and *Discovery*;

Franklin's *Erebus* and *Terror*;
the Hudson Bay Company

on their way to Canadian furs.
The well was sealed in 1931.

I can nearly call you now.
Cars clack and thunder on

the streets paved with sandstone:
Old Hamnavoe not famous for

herring, whaling and war:
beneath Brinkie's Brae

Stromness thrives on the ferry
on tourists like me.

I check the time:
it's *Resolution* and *Discovery*.

The sandstone is grey
as houses. Sea and sky grey

often, too, but these summer days
the sky tints pastel blue,

the sea a depth-dark rippling
blue. Your eye-colour.

Your humour, too. Someone
has named the street that climbs

the Brae the Khyber Pass.
I check the time again:

Erebus and *Terror*.
So are you awake yet?

Are you dreaming of me?
I've found Graham Place

here, which doesn't mean
I don't miss you. No,

I think it means
I'm coming home.

Acknowledgments

I would like to thank the editors of the following publications where these poems first appeared, sometimes in very different versions.

Magazines:

The Alsop Review: "On Skye," "Tomb of the Eagles"

Arc: "Wearing Nothing But the Midnight Sun" (Confederation Poets Prize)

Canadian Literature: "Aged Black, Morning Green: Edinburgh," "Hunting The Lady Well: Near Rosemarkie, The Black Isle"

Cascadia Subduction Zone: "What I Mean When I Talk About Ruins"

Dream Catcher (U.K.): "Atlantic Pacific"

Full Unit Hookup: "Lockerbie"

Goblin Fruit: "Westron Wind"

Grain: "Carnasserie Castle"

Interfictions: "Aucindrain Inventory: Village Museum"

Lady Churchill's Rosebud Wristlet: "Hermitage," "Machrie Moor," "The Tattoos I Don't Have," "Westness Walk: Rousay"

LitRag: "1773," "The Grey Cairns of Camster"

Lynx: Poetry from Bath: "By Road By Ruin" as "The Cairn by the Road," "Dwarfie Stane, Isle of Hoy"

The Malahat Review: "Egg and Sky Skye and Egg," "Giants Graves Forest Trail[1] Painted by Numbers"

Museletter: "On Skye"

Prairie Fire: "Petraphilia"

Prism International: "Tomb of the Eagles"

Queen's Quarterly: "3 St Ronan's Drive"

Red-Headed Stepchild: "How To Explore The Land of Your Ancestors"

Stone's Throw Magazine: "Inchcolm Abbey"

Thin Air: "The Scrawlings: Maes Howe" as a section of "The Mainland Tour: Orkney"

Tickle Ace: "The Walk She Takes: Smailholm Tower"

Anthologies:

The Alsop Review Anthology One: "Graves and Churchyards Cairns and Cairns," "The Walk She Takes," "Wearing Nothing But The Midnight Sun"

And No One Knows the Blood We Share: Poems from the Feminist Caucus: "On Skye"

Letters to the World: Poems from the Wom-Po Listserv: "On Skye"

Long Journey: Pacific Northwest Poets: "The Walk She Takes: Smailholm Tower" and "Graves and Churchyards Cairns and Cairns"

Poets West: "Dwarfie Stane: Isle of Hoy", "On Skye"

Pontoon 4: "Kilmichael Glassary"

Vintage 93: "Tomb of the Eagles" (honorable mention, League of Canadian Poets National Poetry Contest)

Vintage 95: "On Skye", (Third Prize, National Poetry Contest, League of Canadian Poets), "Walking The Land's Edge" (honorable mention, National Poetry Contest, League of Canadian's Poets)

My gratitude to Lana Ayers and MoonPath Press for giving this book a home and a physical and electronic being.

I would like to thank my fellow explorers, Christina DeCoursey, Matt DeCoursey, Shelagh & John Graham, James Gurley, and Jens Tagore Brage, for care and companionship on my various tours of Scotland. John Barton, Ruth Brinton, Elaine Chukan Brown, Vicki Ford, James Gurley, Therese Quig, Harold Rhenisch, and Janet Sekijima gave invaluable editorial advice. Karen Fishler helped me keep faith, Devin Gurley and Mark Gurley kept in touch, and Tamar Boursalian helped the poems come alive in the recordings for *She Says: Poems Selected and New*. Thanks to Anne Chafee for the last-minute scanner and to Jae Steinbacher for the last-minute copyedit.

Special thanks to John Barclay Graham for sparking my love of Scotland and of stone, to Jocelyn Harrold for her genealogical work, and to James Gurley for all the inspiration and being the one I come home to.

Much of this book is in conversation with Robin Skelton's *Timelight* and Richard Hugo's *The Right Madness on Skye*, and it was outside Dick's office door that Jim and I met. Much of this book is in conversation with no longer being in any way young.

I am immensely grateful to the Canada Council and the King County Arts Commission for support during the writing of these poems.

About the Author

Neile Graham's paternal grandparents met on the ship as they immigrated from Scotland to Canada, and her maternal grandfather was also born in Scotland, though her maternal grandmother was of Sassenach (English) heritage. She herself was born in Winnipeg, Manitoba, Canada and grew up in Victoria, B.C. Educated at the universities of Victoria and Montana, she works at the College of Built Environments of the University of Washington and lives in Seattle, but has visited her ancestral home frequently. She is also a graduate of the Clarion West Writers Workshop for writers of speculative fiction and served as its workshop administrator, then as workshop director.

Her poetry, short fiction, reviews, and nonfiction have been published in American, British, and Canadian literary journals and anthologies. She has three previous collections: *Seven Robins*; *Spells for Clear Vision*, which was shortlisted for the Pat Lowther Memorial Award for the best book of poems by a Canadian woman; *Blood Memory*; and a selection of spoken word recordings, *She Says: Poems Selected and New*.

She has appeared at the Bumbershoot Arts Festival and served as Writer-in-Residence for the Virginia Highlands

Arts Festival, and her work has been supported by grants from the Canada Council, Artist Trust, and the Seattle, King County, and Washington State arts commissions. She won *Arc* magazine's Confederation Poets Prize, placed third in the League of Canadian Poets' National Poetry Contest, and has been nominated multiple times for the Rhysling Award and *Arc*'s Poem of the Year contest. Her work has also been included in Chizine's *Imaginarium* series of the best of Canadian speculative fiction and poetry. In 2017 she won the World Fantasy Award, Special Award Non-Professional "for fostering excellence in the genre through her role as Workshop Director, Clarion West." See neilegraham.com for more information.

CPSIA information can be obtained
at www.ICGtesting.com
Printed in the USA
FSHW011946051119
63805FS